A~~lberto~~saurus: Big animal.

THE EAGLE-EYED EXPLORER CLUB

AGENT EAGLE,

For reasons we cannot reveal, an urgent investigation into the World of the Dinosaurs must be carried out.

Go back to the prehistoric past and uncover every detail of the dinosaurs' story.

Submit your field notes detailing such matters as dinosaur identification, diversity and extinction via the club's secret postbox. Include a timeline with facts and sketches on more than 100 dinosaurs. Return all documents no later than ~~██████████~~

Warning: this expedition is full of danger. We hope it will not be your last. Look up, look out and don't get too close to a Velociraptor.

Go carefully!

I'm Eric Eagle, Senior Librarian of the Eagle-Eyed Explorer Club. Years ago, the club recruited me as one of its special agents — codename, Agent Eagle.

Most days you'll find me in the basement of the library, organising the atlases. But I always keep my rucksack at the ready, in case the club needs me for one of its urgent missions. I never know when to expect a call.

My latest mission is not only top secret, but very dangerous, so keep it hush-hush. The club has ordered me to file a report on the entire history of the dinosaurs as soon as possible. It looks like I'll need to go back millions of years in time.

1. DINOSAUR IDENTIFICATION

NYASASAURUS

'Dinosaurs were ancient types of reptile, distant cousins to modern reptiles, such as lizards. They lived on the Earth for 176 million years. That's hard to comprehend for humans like us, who have only been around for less than 200,000 years. What clues have been found about the oldest known dinosaur? Who first discovered the dinosaurs? Where does the name "dinosaur" come from? And how do you identify a dinosaur fossil?'

Mysterious clues in ancient bones

Our expedition into the history of the dinosaurs starts on the sandy shores of Lake Malawi in southern Tanzania, Africa.

Here, in the 1930s, palaeontologists (scientists who study ancient living things) found a curious cluster of bones that was not so easy to identify: one single arm bone and several pieces of vertebrae (backbone).

A ridge along the arm indicated that whatever the creature was, it was strong, with powerful muscles. And although the bones looked like those of a reptile, their structure was more like a bird or mammal skeleton. Above its hips, three vertebrae were fused together, unlike modern reptiles, which just have two. What sort of creature did the bones belong to?

Different scientists, much later on in 2012, came to an exciting conclusion. They had seen these types of clues before and knew what they were looking at. What had been found was ancient, what had been found was unique – it was a dinosaur!

Nyasasaurus, as the mysterious creature was named, is now thought to be the oldest dinosaur ever discovered, living about 240 million years ago in the Triassic period.

The unidentified reptilian bones

A history of discovery

Nyasasaurus may be the oldest dinosaur ever found, but people have been unearthing fossil evidence of dinosaurs for a long time. In 1676, in Oxfordshire, people dug up the bones of an animal far larger than any creature then alive. No one knew what the bones belonged to. Some said they were elephant bones, left behind by the Romans. Others said they came from a giant human from biblical times.

It was not until 1822 that the British palaeontologist William Buckland suggested that the bones, which included a giant tooth, may have belonged to a creature he called *Megalosaurus*, a huge but extinct reptile!

William Buckland – dinosaur hunter

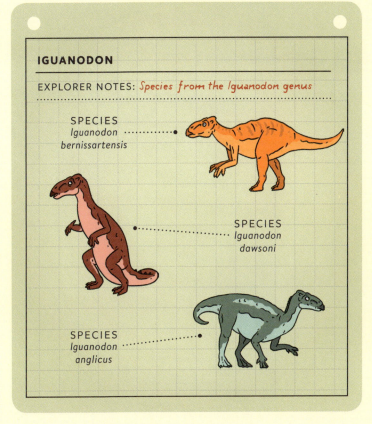

IGUANODON

EXPLORER NOTES: *Species from the Iguanodon genus*

SPECIES *Iguanodon bernissartensis*

SPECIES *Iguanodon dawsoni*

SPECIES *Iguanodon anglicus*

New names for prehistoric fossils

Twenty years later, British biologist Richard Owen identified similarities between *Megalosaurus* and fossils of *Iguanodon* and *Hyaleosaurus*. It was his idea that they all belonged to a group of extinct reptiles he called *Dinosauria*, meaning 'terrible lizard'. But, the dinosaurs were not lizards, and they were not all terrible either!

Biologists give scientific names to different animals or plants to show how they are connected. A group of living things that share certain characteristics is called a 'genus'. But different individuals within the group may have further differences of their own. This is where the word 'species' comes in. Dinosaurs in the genus *Iguanodon* share certain traits, but *Iguanodon dawsoni* is its own species – a specific type of *Iguanodon* with its own specific characteristics.

'Turn the page to discover how dinosaur fossils are identified!'

DINOSAUR IDENTIFICATION

What does a dinosaur look like?

Dinosaurs evolved into all sorts of shapes and sizes, so palaeontologists have to look very carefully when identifying a fossil. *Giganotosaurus* was a huge predator, with razor-sharp teeth and two powerful hind legs. *Lambeosaurus* had a large crest on its head, perhaps to amplify its calls to potential mates. *Argentinosaurus* walked on all fours and had a long neck, stretching a massive 30 metres from head to tail. Other dinosaurs were relatively tiny – *Compsognathus* was a metre long – possibly the perfect size to catch lizards in the undergrowth.

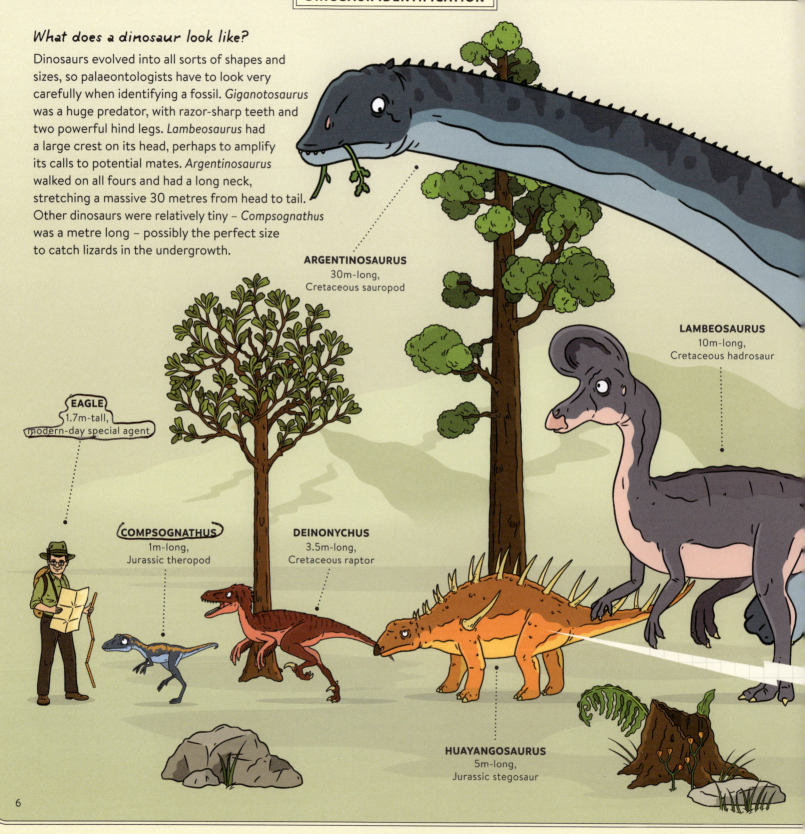

ARGENTINOSAURUS
30m-long, Cretaceous sauropod

LAMBEOSAURUS
10m-long, Cretaceous hadrosaur

EAGLE
1.7m-tall, modern-day special agent

COMPSOGNATHUS
1m-long, Jurassic theropod

DEINONYCHUS
3.5m-long, Cretaceous raptor

HUAYANGOSAURUS
5m-long, Jurassic stegosaur

DINOSAUR IDENTIFICATION

How do you know it's a dinosaur?

You can tell if a fossil might come from a dinosaur by comparing it to the skeletons of reptiles today. Modern reptiles such as tortoises or Komodo dragons have legs that stick out sideways as they crawl along. But dinosaurs' legs always point straight down. Straight legs may have helped predators such as *Deinonychus* run swiftly after their prey, but they are also a useful clue to help palaeontologists decide whether they have discovered a dinosaur!

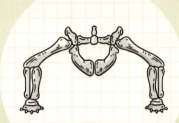

MODERN REPTILE LEGS

DINOSAUR LEGS

GIGANOTOSAURUS
13m-long, Cretaceous theropod

What's the great dinosaur divide?

Dinosaurs are divided into two groups with different shaped hip bones. A fossil's hips show how dinosaurs might be related. Dinosaurs such as *Huayangosaurus* are grouped as 'ornithiscians', meaning 'bird-hipped'. Dinosaurs such as *Giganotosaurus* are grouped as 'saurischians', which means 'lizard-hipped'. No one really knows why these two groups evolved differently, and it is a question scientists are still exploring.

ORNITHISCHIAN HIP BONES

SAURISCHIAN HIP BONES

2. DINOSAUR LIVES

LILIENSTERNUS

'We've learned how palaeontologists identify fossils. But to really understand the dinosaurs, we must investigate their lives more closely. We begin in the Triassic period, 240 million years ago, when dinosaurs first emerged. What was the world like for the dinosaurs at that time? What rivals posed a threat? As the world began to change, did the dinosaurs change too? And, over time, what did the dinosaurs eat — or were they the ones being eaten?'

Welcome to the Triassic

Our explorations start on the southern edges of 'Pangaea', the name given to the giant continent that made up all the land on Earth during the Triassic period. As time passed, Pangaea broke up and new continents formed, with parts of Pangaea's southern expanses eventually becoming South America and Africa today.

The extreme temperatures at Pangaea's centre were challenging for the creatures that lived on the supercontinent. In the coastal regions however, the air was cooler. Humid forests of conifers and ferns grew along Pangaea's edges. Among the leaves and low-hanging branches, early dinosaurs like *Eoraptor* were on the prowl. A small, metre-long meat-eater, *Eoraptor* lived on Pangaea 230 million years ago. It was a biped, meaning it walked on two legs. It had a slim, lightweight body and a long tail that helped it balance as it darted after its prey.

Around 10 million years later, you might have seen other nimble, long-tailed bipedal dinosaurs, such as *Liliensternus*, about to eat its next meal. On its head it had a distinctive, eye-catching crest, and in its mouth there might have been a small reptile, a favourite snack for some Triassic meat-eaters!

The Triassic world

All change!

As we have discovered, most early dinosaurs were small, two-legged hunters. But millions of years later, some dinosaurs had four legs (quadrupeds) and long necks, while others had sails on their backs. This diversity reveals evolution at work.

Evolution is a process of change that takes place slowly, where creatures' bodies adapt in ways that help them survive. These adaptations happen when genes passing down the generations accidentally alter. Genes are the instructions guiding the growth of every living thing – your own body is full of them!

For example, one adaptation might lead to a species evolving with stronger jaws for hunting, while their arms and fingers become weaker with time as they are no longer used to catch prey. Individuals with useful genes have a better chance of survival and produce offspring with the same successful genetic code. Those that don't adapt will eventually die out.

Coelophysis vs. Postosuchus

Reptilian rivalry

Early dinosaurs like *Eoraptor* and *Liliensternus* were probably swift hunters, but they were not at the top of the Triassic food chain. Bigger, more powerful reptiles dominated, and probably even ate dinosaurs as part of their diet!

One such reptile was *Postosuchus*. A huge, powerful predator with gnarled, scaly skin, more closely related to today's crocodiles than to the dinosaurs, *Postosuchus* could grow up to five metres long, twice the length of the biggest early dinosaurs. Even larger Triassic dinosaurs, such as 2.5-metre-long *Coelophysis*, would have had little chance against *Postosuchus*'s huge jaws and teeth.

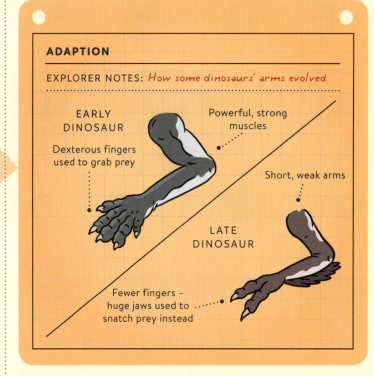

ADAPTION

EXPLORER NOTES: *How some dinosaurs' arms evolved*

EARLY DINOSAUR — Dexterous fingers used to grab prey — Powerful, strong muscles

LATE DINOSAUR — Short, weak arms — Fewer fingers – huge jaws used to snatch prey instead

'Turn the page to discover how dinosaur diets changed over time!'

DINOSAUR LIVES

How did dinosaur diets change?

A decent meal is essential for survival. Dinosaurs in the early Triassic were generally small, quick and carnivorous (meat-eating). But gradually, the Earth's atmosphere began to change, encouraging the growth of more plants and trees. As the world changed, the dinosaurs adapted too, and many herbivorous (plant-eating) species evolved and fed on this new greenery. Some dinosaurs ate both plants and meat. They are called 'omnivores'. In my notes, we can take a closer look at different ways dinosaurs evolved, to make sure they never went hungry.

HERRERASAURUS | TRIASSIC | CARNIVEROUS

EXPLORER NOTES: *Had serrated teeth for tearing into flesh*

Although large for the Triassic period, six-metre-long bipedal *Herrerasaurus* was a lean, agile predator, and like other early dinosaurs, was a fast mover. If it spotted a potential meal – a smaller reptile or even another dinosaur – it would have sprung, grabbing it with its three pairs of claws, before baring its sharp, serrated teeth and taking a bite.

TIMELINE DATE *231 million years ago*

PLATEOSAURUS | TRIASSIC | HERBIVOROUS

EXPLORER NOTES: *Used a four-metre-long neck to reach tall trees*

In the late Triassic, when some dinosaurs were still scampering around the forest floor eating lizards, other plant-eating dinosaurs had evolved to much larger proportions. If ten-metre-long quadruped *Plateosaurus* stood on its hind legs, it would have been taller than a two-storey house! It could use its long neck to reach the branches in tall trees, while its large stomach helped it digest all those leaves.

TIMELINE DATE *214 million years ago*

BRACHIOSAURUS | JURASSIC | HERBIVOROUS

EXPLORER NOTES: *Stewed up tough plants in its big belly*

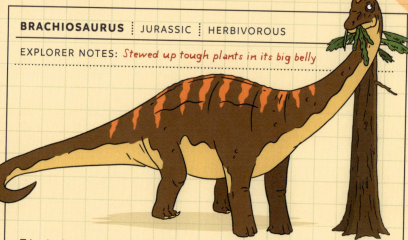

Triassic dinosaur *Plateosaurus* may have had a long neck, but Jurassic *Brachiosaurus* went one – or rather two – steps further, with two front legs that were longer than its hind limbs. This adaptation, along with its nine-metre-long neck, helped this 25-metre-long quadruped reach tasty leaves high up in the forest canopy. Despite its weak teeth, *Brachiosaurus* had a powerful gut and spent weeks digesting – or 'fermenting' – its meals to get all the healthy nutrients out of its greens.

TIMELINE DATE *154 million years ago*

DINOSAUR LIVES

HETERODONTOSAURUS : JURASSIC : OMNIVOROUS

EXPLORER NOTES: *Chopped, chewed and ground its food*

This 1.5-metre-long bipedal dinosaur had a sharp beak to help it chop leaves off plants, which was useful in the leafy Jurassic period. Its firm front teeth could chew on plants, and it could grind each bite thoroughly with its powerful molars. But what if leaves were not on the menu? Heterodontosaurus was an omnivore and perhaps used its tusk-like front teeth to tear into a termite mound and feast on a mountain of insects instead.

TIMELINE DATE *195 million years ago*

TROODON : CRETACEOUS : OMNIVOROUS

EXPLORER NOTES: *Had a big brain that probably helped it outsmart prey*

Sharp teeth helped some dinosaurs rip into their prey, while a big long neck meant others could reach up to fresh leaves. But occasionally it helped to just stop and think. Troodon's brain was quite big for its 2.5-metre length, and palaeontologists suggest it had above-average intelligence for a dinosaur, as well as excellent vision. It may have been a shrewd hunter that could spot another small Cretaceous animal, wait, and then at the right moment slash out with its sharp sickle-like claw.

TIMELINE DATE *75 million years ago*

NIGERSAURUS : CRETACEOUS : HERBIVOROUS

EXPLORER NOTES: *Used a vacuum-cleaner-shaped skull lined with 100 teeth to hoover up plants*

Nigersaurus's mouth was so full of teeth, it's a wonder that it could actually fit any food in there at all! This nine-metre-long quadruped's jaws were lined with 100 teeth, with up to eight replacements per tooth. Its flat-fronted skull was especially adapted to sucking up food from the forest floor, and if it lost a tooth, there was always another in reserve.

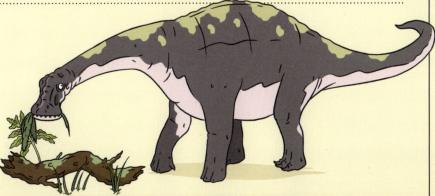

TIMELINE DATE *105 million years ago*

3. DINOSAUR SURVIVAL

STEGOSAURUS

'When dinosaurs first emerged in the Triassic 240 million years ago, many were small and at risk of being eaten by other reptiles. Yet by the end of the Jurassic period, 95 million years later, they had evolved in ways that enabled them to completely dominate life on Earth. What was life like in the Jurassic? How did dinosaurs spread across the globe? How do dinosaur eggs fit into the story? Over time, how did dinosaurs evolve and adapt to new conditions?'

The Jurassic world

By the beginning of the Jurassic period, the Earth's climate had become milder and wetter. The supercontinent of Pangaea had split in two, forming one giant land-mass called Gondwana, in the south, and another, called Laurasia, in the north. Ocean waters filled the gulfs between them.

Jurassic dinosaurs were residents of this new world. The rocky expanses of the Triassic had retreated, and green strands of ferns and conifers spread over the Earth. In every corner, dinosaur life flourished.

An abundance of new plant life and vegetation meant some Jurassic dinosaurs evolved into much larger sizes, compared to the early species. *Diplodocus*, a long-necked, plant-eating sauropod, grew to a massive 27 metres in length – its huge bulk might have offered some protection against attack.

A great number of different species emerged, with new characteristics that may have helped them survive. Four-legged *Stegosaurus* had large plates on its back and a spiked tail. The plates may have scared away predators, or even helped to attract partners. In the changing temperatures on Earth at that time, the plates may have also kept *Stegosaurus* cool in the sunlight or warm in the shade.

From pole to pole

Although armoured plates may have ensured dinosaurs like *Stegosaurus* survived, there may be another reason why they were able to spread so successfully across the globe. At the end of the Triassic, competing reptile groups and other creatures died out in a mass extinction, perhaps due to changes in the world's atmosphere. These creatures' food and habitats were now freely available to the dinosaurs, and, unchallenged by rivals, they slowly began to fill in the gaps, dominating the globe, from pole to pole.

Apex predator, Allosaurus, on the attack

As the plant-eating dinosaurs grew larger, some meat-eaters did too, and they evolved in ways that helped them hunt larger prey. These dinosaurs were apex predators and included powerful 12-metre-long *Allosaurus*, a viciously toothed meat-eater. When it caught sight of a lone plant-eater, it might have charged head first, swinging its powerful skull towards its terrified victim.

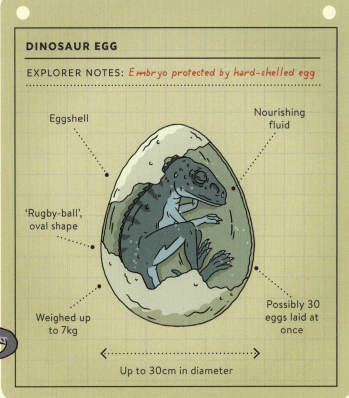

DINOSAUR EGG

EXPLORER NOTES: *Embryo protected by hard-shelled egg*

- Eggshell
- Nourishing fluid
- 'Rugby-ball', oval shape
- Weighed up to 7kg
- Possibly 30 eggs laid at once

Up to 30cm in diameter

The secret power of eggs

Dinosaurs, like *Allosaurus*, ruled over life for millions of years, and their success could have much to do with something as simple as an eggshell! Like birds and other reptiles, dinosaurs were egg-layers. An egg's shell stops the embryo inside from drying out, meaning dinosaurs could lay their eggs anywhere in hot climates, away from the water, improving the next generation's chances of surviving.

Some dinosaurs may have been very protective parents too, who cared for their young. At a site named 'Egg Mountain' in the USA, palaeontologists discovered fossilised dinosaur eggs grouped together in different nests all in one spot. This suggests that perhaps some dinosaurs gathered to lay their eggs in large colonies.

'Turn the page to discover how dinosaurs' bodies evolved, helping ensure their survival!'

DINOSAUR SURVIVAL

How did scales help dinosaurs survive?

Over millions of years, as the environment changed, dinosaurs' bodies evolved and adapted. The Triassic world could be a dangerous place, bumps and scrapes might easily lead to life-threatening infections or dehydration. Scaly skin, which seals in moisture, first emerged with the dinosaurs' reptilian ancestors and helped combat such challenges. Early Triassic dinosaurs like *Pisanosaurus* had scaly skin, an evolutionary development still seen on lizards and snakes today.

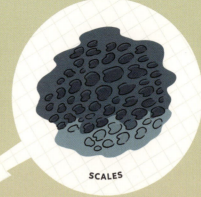

SCALES

PISANOSAURUS
Scaly,
Triassic ornithischian

Did dinosaurs have feathers?

The process of evolution is happening all the time. As species are influenced by their changing environment, new adaptations develop that may help them prosper. After examining a *Tianyulong* fossil from the Jurassic, palaeontologists noted a line of long quills along its back. These 'proto-feathers' were an early form of the feathers that evolved on many dinosaurs later on, perhaps to attract mates or maybe to help keep them warm.

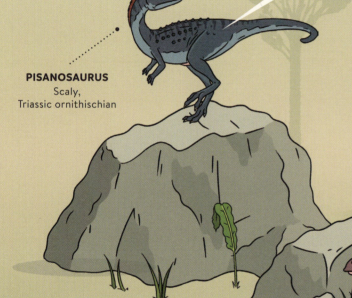

TIANYULONG
Feathered,
Jurassic heterodontosaurid

FEATHERS

DINOSAUR SURVIVAL

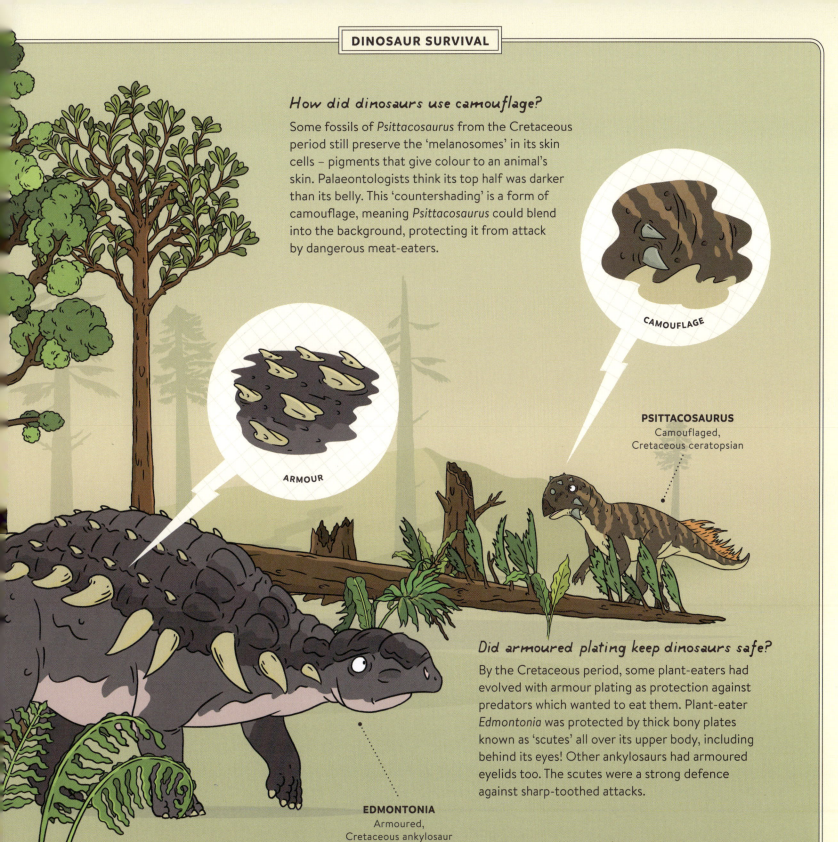

How did dinosaurs use camouflage?

Some fossils of *Psittacosaurus* from the Cretaceous period still preserve the 'melanosomes' in its skin cells – pigments that give colour to an animal's skin. Palaeontologists think its top half was darker than its belly. This 'countershading' is a form of camouflage, meaning *Psittacosaurus* could blend into the background, protecting it from attack by dangerous meat-eaters.

CAMOUFLAGE

ARMOUR

PSITTACOSAURUS
Camouflaged,
Cretaceous ceratopsian

Did armoured plating keep dinosaurs safe?

By the Cretaceous period, some plant-eaters had evolved with armour plating as protection against predators which wanted to eat them. Plant-eater *Edmontonia* was protected by thick bony plates known as 'scutes' all over its upper body, including behind its eyes! Other ankylosaurs had armoured eyelids too. The scutes were a strong defence against sharp-toothed attacks.

EDMONTONIA
Armoured,
Cretaceous ankylosaur

4. DINOSAUR DIVERSITY

SPINOSAURUS

EAGLE-EYED LIBRARY · No. 01

'The Cretaceous period began 145 million years ago. There were more dinosaurs alive at that time than ever before, and they continued to dominate life across the planet. The warm and wet climate of the Jurassic continued, but had anything in the dinosaurs' environment changed? Why did competition mean the dinosaurs continued to diversify? What exactly was a "titanosaur"? And what was so unique about the Cretaceous dinosaurs?'

Onward into the Cretaceous

By the beginning of the Cretaceous, Gondwana and Laurasia had split farther apart, and land on Earth was arranged much like the continents are today.

The Cretaceous atmosphere was heavy and humid. In many regions, waterways and marshes criss-crossed the landscape, and plant life flourished. For the first time, small pale petals of flowers were visible, and curious green pods were hanging from the trees, as fruits began to ripen – a new food source for dinosaurs and other Cretaceous animals.

Palaeontologists have found fossil after fossil of distinct species from the Cretaceous and consider it an age of great dinosaur diversity as many new species developed – dinosaurs ruled the world!

Giganotosaurus was an enormous meat-eater. At five metres tall, smaller creatures would have quivered in its shadow, before it crushed them with its massive jaws! *Spinosaurus* is another example of just how unusual Cretaceous dinosaurs could be, with its huge size, measuring 18 metres from head to tail, and a big sail that ran the length of its spine. It lived on dry land as well as in swampy water and had a narrow skull like a crocodile's, with a long, pointed snout, which it used to snap up fish.

The Cretaceous world

Cretaceous competition

The unique body of *Spinosaurus* shows the different ways in which Cretaceous dinosaurs evolved. With so many new species emerging, there was even more competition for food and space, which gradually led to greater diversity as dinosaurs adapted to find their own place or 'niche' within their environment where they could thrive.

Some duck-billed hadrosaurs evolved to feed as a herd, for example, possibly using their head crests to make sounds to warn each other if predators appeared. Such predators might have included ten-metre-long *Albertosaurus*. This meat-eater perhaps also fed as a group, with individuals hunting as a pack, before closing in for the kill.

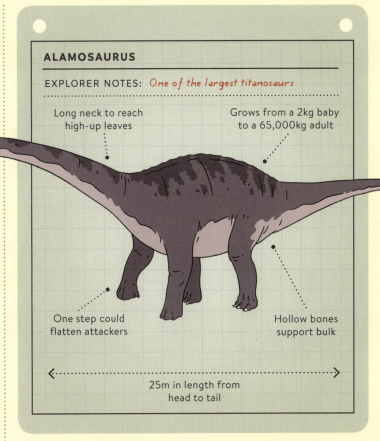

ALAMOSAURUS

EXPLORER NOTES: *One of the largest titanosaurs*

- Long neck to reach high-up leaves
- Grows from a 2kg baby to a 65,000kg adult
- One step could flatten attackers
- Hollow bones support bulk

25m in length from head to tail

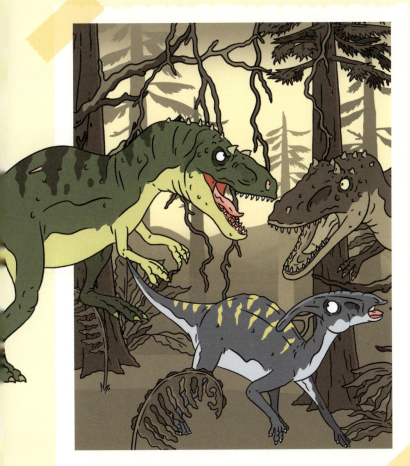

A pack of Albertosaurus *hunt down a hadrosaur*

Giant titanosaurs

Some Cretaceous meat-eaters were so large, they had no need to fear other dinosaurs. But even a pack of bulky *Albertosaurus* may have scattered in alarm if they heard the footsteps of an approaching *Alamosaurus*. It was a giant plant-eating sauropod, one of a group of dinosaurs palaeontologists call 'titanosaurs'. Some of them were simply big, but others were gigantic – *Alamosaurus* was 25 metres in length, over double the size of powerful meat-eaters like *Albertosaurus* and *T. rex*.

Other titanosaurs were even larger – *Argentinosaurus* weighed 70 tonnes and was 30 metres long. No land animals before or since have ever grown so enormous!

'Turn the page to discover what was unique about the Cretaceous dinosaurs!'

DINOSAUR DIVERSITY

What was unique about the Cretaceous dinosaurs?

In the Triassic, dinosaurs tended to look quite similar. However, by the Cretaceous, dinosaurs looked very different from each other – my notes show how diverse different species had become. Some had unique adaptations that helped them protect themselves, others had adaptations that helped them find mates. Some evolved with such bizarre features palaeontologists don't really know what they were for! Different adaptations helped dinosaurs sidestep competitors in the race to survive.

TYRANNOSAURUS REX | 8,000kg | 12m-long

EXPLORER NOTES: Bit prey with 30cm-long teeth

T. rex was one of the most successful Cretaceous predators, not least because its sharp teeth were 30 centimetres long, larger than those of any other dinosaur from any other period. *T. rex* wasn't shy about using them either – close inspection of fossils reveals *T. rex* bite marks on skeletons from all sorts of other dinosaurs. *T. rex* may have been a slow runner for its size, but its remarkable teeth would have made quick work of its prey.

TIMELINE DATE 68 million years ago

TRICERATOPS | 7,000kg | 9m-long

EXPLORER NOTES: Had a 1.8m-wide head shield, probably for showing off

There are many ways the Cretaceous dinosaurs might have caught your attention, but a dinosaur with long spiky horns and a 1.8-metre frilly shield around its head would certainly have stood out from the pack. Horns were good for fighting and a big shield proved effective for defence, but palaeontologists think *Triceratops* might have also have used its unique head shield to attract mates.

TIMELINE DATE 68 million years ago

PARASAUROLOPHUS | 3,000kg | 10m-long

EXPLORER NOTES: May have used a 2m-long crest for communication

Cretaceous plant-eater *Parasaurolophus* had a hollow two-metre crest on its skull. At first, some befuddled researchers thought perhaps it functioned as a giant nose, giving *Parasaurolophus* a super-powered sense of smell for finding food or staying alert to attackers. But when one of them blew air through a model of the crest, a deep honking sound came out. Their new theory is that the striking crest was probably more like a trumpet, helping *Parasaurolophus* call to its herd.

TIMELINE DATE 76 million years ago

DINOSAUR DIVERSITY

PACHYCEPHALOSAURUS | 400kg | 5m-long

EXPLORER NOTES: *Had an enlarged 25cm-thick bony skull, probably for bashing other Pachycephalosaurus*

Pachycephalosaurus was a 'bone-headed' dinosaur. It was a bipedal plant-eater with a rigid crown of spikes surrounding its sizable 25-centimetre-thick skull. Palaeontologists think that in a clearing somewhere in a Cretaceous forest, *Pachycephalosaurus* males may have competed with each other, perhaps for the interest of a passing female, by bashing into each other's bodies with their bony heads.

TIMELINE DATE *68 million years ago*

VELOCIRAPTOR | 15kg | 2m-long

EXPLORER NOTES: *Used 7cm-long claws to slash prey*

Velociraptor was a lean Cretaceous meat-eater, with a long tail it could use for balance as it pounced on prey. Its large brain suggests it was intelligent and its distinctive seven-centimetre-long claws made it a lethal predator. Its large eyes could have easily picked out a victim, and then its sharp claws would have struck with deadly force.

TIMELINE DATE *75 million years ago*

ANKYLOSAURUS | 6,000kg | 6m-long

EXPLORER NOTES: *Swung a 3m-long clubbed tail*

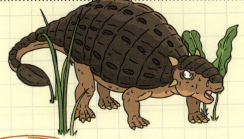

Ankylosaurus was a large, compact Cretaceous plant-eater. Rather than sharp teeth or a big brain, it evolved with an upper body covered in thick bony plates, which might have provided some protection from attack. But if an enemy wouldn't give up, it also had an impressive three-metre-long tail with a thick, bony club at the end, which it could swing and knock its enemies flying!

TIMELINE DATE *67 million years ago*

5. DINOSAUR EXTINCTION

MASS EXTINCTION

'The dinosaurs were the most powerful creatures on Earth for 136 million years. Yet by the late Cretaceous period, 66 million years ago, fossils from dinosaurs and many other creatures as well suddenly disappeared. After millions of years of successful adaption on an ever-changing planet, what catastrophic events caused the dinosaurs to vanish? How did the world change? Why do mass extinctions happen? And why did some species survive, while the dinosaurs died out?'

The K-T mass extinction

The 'K-T extinction', short for Cretaceous-Tertiary, is the name palaeontologists have given to the mass extinction at the end of the Cretaceous period, when 80 per cent of all species on Earth died out, including the dinosaurs.

Scientists are still looking for answers to explain what happened. They think at that time destructive forces were bubbling under the Earth's surface and molten lava poured out of volcanoes in a barren region called the Deccan Traps, in what is India today. Toxic gases leaked into the atmosphere and temperatures dropped severely. These extreme conditions might help to explain why so many creatures died out all at once. On the hunt for further clues, scientists investigated some rocks from the late Cretaceous period. They found traces of a metal called iridium. It hardly ever forms on Planet Earth, but is found in meteorites from Outer Space. The scientists proposed the iridium came from a meteorite that struck the Earth so powerfully that it started a chain reaction, causing huge earthquakes, epic floods and massive environmental destruction. These events unbalanced ecosystems across the world and endangered all forms of life.

Beneath a volcano's surface — Vent, Lava, Ash, Branch pipe, Magma

Why mass extinctions happen

There have been five mass extinction events in prehistory. Usually they are caused by dramatic climate changes, or are sometimes triggered by sudden meteorite strikes, super-volcanoes or ice ages. The End-Permian extinction, about 250 million years ago, resulted in up to 96 per cent of all species dying out. A species becoming extinct may allow others to flourish. The mass extinction at the end of the Triassic helped the dinosaurs go on to become the Earth's top predators, as there was less competition for food and space. Some scientists predict a sixth mass extinction is happening right now, but this one is different, as it is being caused by humans.

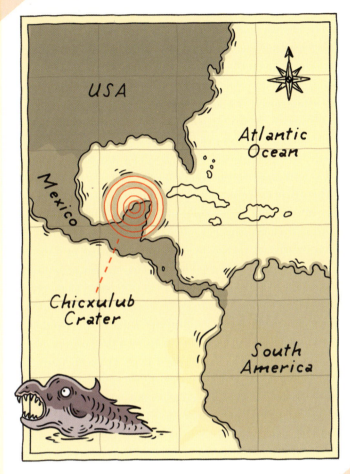

The 177km-wide Chicxulub Crater impact site

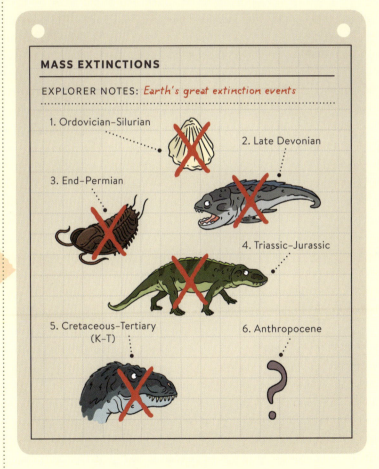

How the world changed

Scientists believe the meteorite smashed into the Earth in a region off the coast of Mexico today. Its impact created a 177-kilometre-wide hole called the Chicxulub Crater, and sent a massive cloud of superheated dust into the atmosphere.

The dust cloud may have hung over the entire planet for years, polluting the rain and blocking out the sun. Without sunlight for warmth or energy, plant life struggled to grow, and without plants, the dinosaurs lost a vital source of food. Combined with the violent Deccan Trap eruptions and sinking global temperatures, the dinosaurs' very existence was under threat, and they slowly became extinct.

'Turn the page to discover why some species survived, but the dinosaurs died out!'

DINOSAUR EXTINCTION

Did the dinosaurs starve to death?

Dinosaurs were the largest land animals the world has ever known, but with their giant size came giant appetites. Due to the unstable environment in the late Cretaceous, the plants that many dinosaurs ate began to disappear. With large amounts of food no longer available, bigger plant-eaters such as *Triceratops* died out. With no plant-eaters left to feed on, meat-eaters such as *T. rex* began to starve. Other giant reptiles, including pterosaurs such as *Quetzalcoatlus*, with its ten-metre wingspan, also vanished.

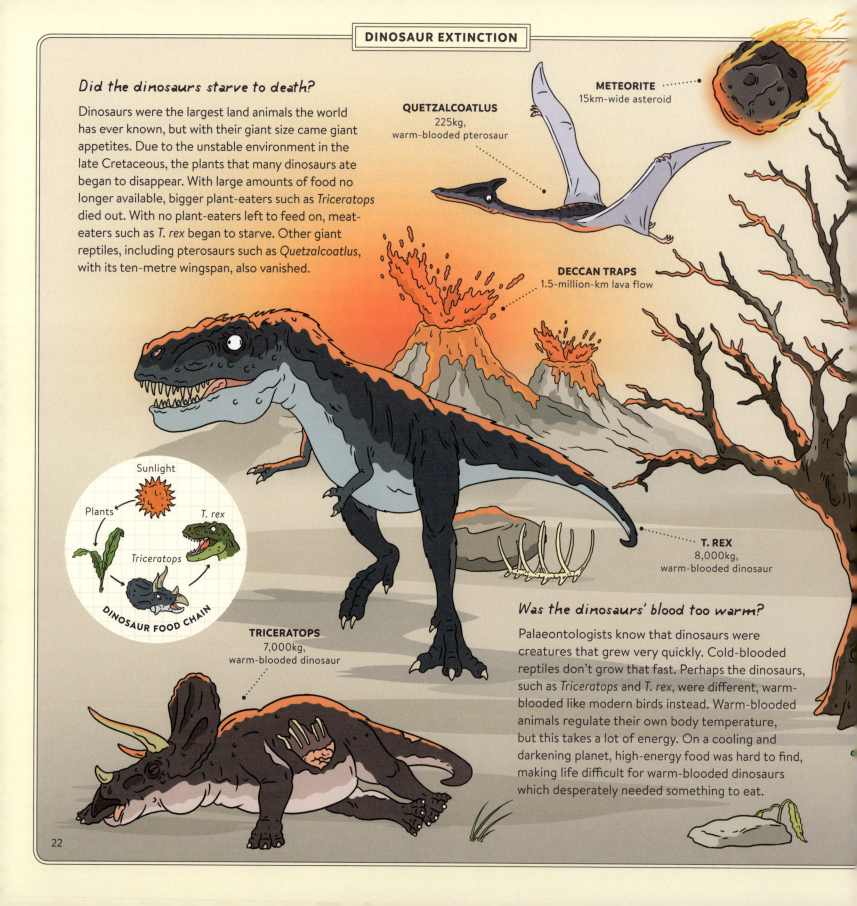

QUETZALCOATLUS
225kg,
warm-blooded pterosaur

METEORITE
15km-wide asteroid

DECCAN TRAPS
1.5-million-km lava flow

T. REX
8,000kg,
warm-blooded dinosaur

TRICERATOPS
7,000kg,
warm-blooded dinosaur

DINOSAUR FOOD CHAIN — Sunlight, Plants, Triceratops, T. rex

Was the dinosaurs' blood too warm?

Palaeontologists know that dinosaurs were creatures that grew very quickly. Cold-blooded reptiles don't grow that fast. Perhaps the dinosaurs, such as *Triceratops* and *T. rex*, were different, warm-blooded like modern birds instead. Warm-blooded animals regulate their own body temperature, but this takes a lot of energy. On a cooling and darkening planet, high-energy food was hard to find, making life difficult for warm-blooded dinosaurs which desperately needed something to eat.

DINOSAUR EXTINCTION

MIACIS
5kg,
warm-blooded mammal

Were the dinosaurs too big?

Mammals, such as the tree-climbing *Miacis*, and birds, such as the goose-like *Presbyornis*, were very small compared to most dinosaurs. As the food chain changed, smaller animals had some key advantages – they needed less food and could live on insects and lizards or fruit. Gradually, as the environment recovered, they were able to flourish in a world the dinosaurs no longer dominated. In fact, today, some of the most successful creatures on Earth are mammals, just like you and me!

EAGLE: PRESENT-DAY MAMMAL

DIDELPHODON
5kg,
warm-blooded mammal

PRESBYORNIS
10kg,
warm-blooded bird

WAIMANU
25kg,
warm-blooded bird

Did the dinosaurs freeze?

As temperatures fell, larger warm-blooded dinosaurs, even those with feathers for warmth, died out. But some creatures endured the cold. Their descendants include lizards, such as *Saniwa*; snakes, such as *Titanoboa*; and crocodilians, such as *Borealosuchus*, whose cold-blooded bodies meant they needed less energy than warm-blooded animals. Small mammals, such as *Didelphodon*, or birds, such as *Waimanu*, although warm-blooded like the dinosaurs, flourished later on, probably thanks to their smaller size and thicker coats.

SANIWA
10kg,
cold-blooded lizard

BOREALOSUCHUS
200kg,
cold-blooded crocodilian

TITANOBOA
1,000kg,
cold-blooded snake

6. DINOSAUR EXCAVATION

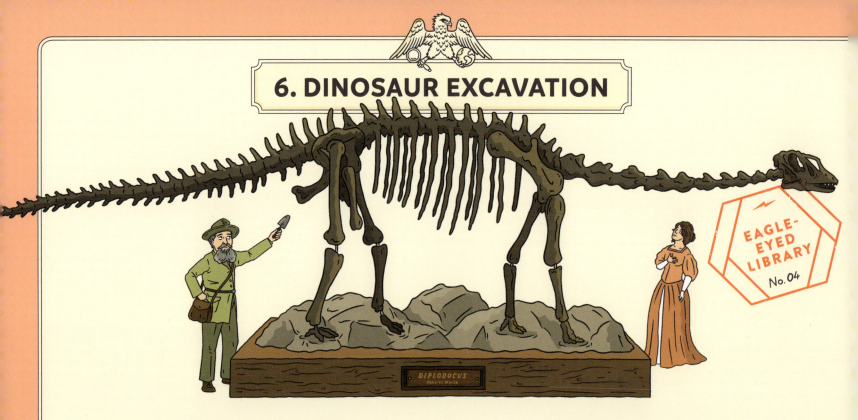

'Humans have long been fascinated by dinosaurs – ever since William Buckland dug up a Megalosaurus skeleton in 1822, we have wanted to know more about these extraordinary creatures that once roamed the Earth. What did people first think about dinosaurs? Where is the best place to look for fossils? How do palaeontologists find dinosaurs? And who are the greatest dinosaur Explorers of all time?'

One, two, three, four, I declare a Bone War!

In the nineteenth century, palaeontologists discovered lots of dinosaur fossils for the first time. The public were excited to know more about these strange skeletons from long ago. Newspapers gossiped about the dinosaur Explorers – dinosaurs were in the headlines!

Othniel Marsh and Edward Drinker Cope were two famous American fossil hunters. They were responsible for identifying hundreds of previously unknown dinosaur species. Dinosaurs such as *Diplodocus* and *Stegosaurus* were given their names by Marsh, who also came up with *Allosaurus*, *Apatosaurus* and many more.

Newspapers fuel dino mania!

Cope's biggest claim to fame is little 2.5-metre-long theropod *Coelophysis*.

In the excitement of the new discoveries, Marsh and Cope became fierce rivals. Their competition became know as the 'Bone Wars'. In 1870, Marsh publicly announced Cope had made an embarrassing mistake – Cope thought the skull of an ancient marine reptile *Elasmosaurus* should go on the end of its tail!

The pair spied on each other, made false accusations and even stole each other's fossils. Sadly, in all this madness, many precious dinosaur remains were destroyed.

The best place to find a fossil

From Chile to China, dinosaurs lived all over the world. Palaeontologists have uncovered fossils everywhere. Here are some top tips for the best places around the globe to find dinosaur bones:

Some of the best spots to find a dinosaur

North America: If it's *Triceratops* or *T. rex* you're after, best get digging here.
South America: Remember the titanosaurs? South America was one of their homes. Massive sauropod *Argentinosaurus* lived here, as did the early dinosaurs *Eoraptor* and *Herrerasaurus*.
Mongolia: Sauropod footprints one-metre-wide have been found in Mongolia's Gobi Desert. Finding a fossil here might be easier than you think, as the ancient bones stay near the desert's sandy surface. Smaller dinosaurs like *Velociraptor* were also native to this region.

Tools of the palaeontological trade

The Earth's surface is made up of rocky layers that have built up over millions of years, trapping fossils of previously living things. When searching for dinosaurs, palaeontologists use geological maps to locate rocks from the Triassic to the Cretaceous periods. They look especially in fossil beds – rocky areas containing many fossils. They break the rocks with geological hammers and chisels, and use a thin spike to prise the fossils out, before carefully wrapping their specimens in cloth and plaster. They then write up their findings by making field notes and sketches of their discoveries.

'Turn the page to discover some of the greatest dinosaur Explorers of all time!'

DINOSAUR EXCAVATION

Who are the great dinosaur Explorers?

A claw. A skull. A prehistoric insect trapped in amber. These are all clues from a time long ago that some innovative Explorers have discovered in their search to know more about the dinosaurs' lives. Whether they looked at fossils or thought about dinosaur behaviour, discovered dinosaur eggs or even studied dinosaur dung, this report would have been impossible to create without their work! Here are my notes on the most famous Explorers who have made it into the Eagle-Eyed Explorer's Club Hall of Fame.

BARNUM BROWN | 1873–1963

EXPLORER NOTES: *Dug up the king of dinosaurs*

American fossil fanatic, Barnum Brown loved dinosaurs. He dug up dinosaurs, wrote about dinosaurs, even gave lectures on dinosaurs. His passion for finding dino bones began at a young age, when he spotted fossils as coal miners worked nearby. He made his name as an amateur palaeontologist in 1902 as the first person to uncover the remains of a *T. rex*, which soon got the world digging for dinos.

ROY CHAPMAN ANDREWS | 1884–1960

EXPLORER NOTES: *First to uncover dino eggs*

Roy Chapman Andrews started out as a janitor at the American Museum of Natural History, but went on to become the museum's director and the first Explorer to discover fossilised dinosaur eggs! He found eggs near an *Oviraptor* fossil and presumed the *Oviraptor* had stolen them. Andrews died before learning the eggs belonged to *Oviraptor* itself.

ROBERT T. BAKKER | b.1945

EXPLORER NOTES: *Recognised dinosaurs as clever and complex animals*

Fossils tell us what dinosaurs must have looked like, but Robert T. Bakker, from New Jersey, is interested in what they actually *did*. Bakker sugggests dinosaurs, such as *Deinonychus*, were agile, warm-blooded and might have behaved like many animals in the wild today. He has studied how dinosaurs may have looked after their young, hunted together in packs or migrated when they needed to find food. Bakker's ideas are very different from the old-fashioned view of dinosaurs as slow, blundering beasts.

DINOSAUR EXCAVATION

JACK HORNER | b.1946

EXPLORER NOTES: *Suggested dinosaurs cared for their young*

Some palaeontologists assumed the small dinosaur skeletons they found near larger fossils were different species. But Jack Horner, from Montana, thought otherwise. He proposed the idea of dinosaur families and suggested the smaller fossils were the larger animals' offspring. He discovered evidence of a nesting ground near fossils of *Maiasaura* (a name which means 'good mother lizard'), and showed how this duck-billed dinosaur may have cared for her young, just as a mother duck looks after her ducklings.

SUE HENDRICKSON | b.1949

EXPLORER NOTES: *Found 'Sue', the largest T. rex to date*

Sue Hendrickson, from Illinois, travels everywhere to learn about dinosaurs. In a mine in South America, she came across her first fossil – an insect preserved in amber. Inspired, she returned home to the USA, and kept digging. She found more fossils, including the most complete *T. rex* skeleton ever unearthed. The giant *T. rex* now stands in Chicago's Field Museum. The museum named it 'Sue' after Hendrickson herself.

KAREN CHIN | b.1952

EXPLORER NOTES: *Expert on dinosaur doo-doo*

Some scientists look at dinosaurs' skulls. Others look at their claws or teeth. But fossilised skeletons aren't the only things that remain. In her unique research at the University of Colorado, Karen Chin investigates dinosaur coprolites, the polite name for fossilised dino doo-doo! Just as park rangers can track an animal by following its droppings, Chin has tracked a dinosaur's diet through dung that has been left behind.

7. DINOSAURS TODAY

ARCHAEOPTERYX

EAGLE-EYED LIBRARY No. 06

'Palaeontologists had concluded that the dinosaurs died out due to the environmental catastrophes at the end of the Cretaceous period, 66 million years ago. But then an astonishing discovery changed everything. Perhaps some dinosaurs survived after all — perhaps they even exist today! What was this peculiar discovery? How are ancient reptiles related to birds? What can prehistoric birds tell us? And what have today's birds inherited from the dinosaurs?'

A peculiar fossil

When a strange 150-million-year-old fossil that looked more like a bird than a dinosaur was discovered in 1861, it puzzled palaeontologists. Some did not believe it was real. But the remains were genuine, and the late Jurassic fossil was given the name of *Archaeopteryx*.

Archaeopteryx had feathers like a bird, wings like a bird and a beak like a bird. But in its beak it had teeth, on its wings were sharp claws and at the back, it had a long tail — features more typical of a dinosaur. *Archaeopteryx* may have been one of the earliest dinosaurs to use its feathers for flight, just like modern birds.

Archaeopteryx's toothed dinosaur beak

At first glance, birds and dinosaurs might not seem to be related. But palaeontologists now see things differently. In fact, they think *Archaeopteryx* represents an 'in-between' animal, with characteristics that show the connections between dinosaurs and birds. They consider birds today to be 'avian dinosaurs' (bird-like dinosaurs), descendants of some feathered dinosaurs that survived the K–T extinction.

Over time, certain dinosaurs evolved into modern birds — and whether a seagull or a sparrow, a parrot or a penguin — all modern birds are types of dinosaur!

THEROPODS

EXPLORER NOTES: *How dinosaurs and birds are related*

Eoraptor: early, bipedal dinosaur

THEROPODS
Coelophysis: small, bipedal dinosaur

NON-AVIAN THEROPODS
T. rex: giant, bipedal dinosaur

AVIAN THEROPODS
Chicken: small, modern-day, bipedal avian dinosaur

Ancient reptiles to modern birds

Avian dinosaurs – or modern birds – continue to flourish all over the world. A tiny sparrow might seem very different from a huge ancient reptile, but palaeontologists believe that birds evolved from a group of dinosaurs called 'theropods'. Non-avian theropods such as *Velociraptor* represent one part of this group, avian theropods (including modern birds) another.

A closer look reveals the similarities – ferocious predator *Velociraptor* had a body shape very similar to a bird's. Many theropods had feathers too. Small Cretaceous *Confuciusornis* had a bird-shaped body and even a toothless beak. Over millions of years, as their bodies were influenced by environmental conditions, some dinosaurs evolved into the birds we know today. It's hard to believe, but *T. rex* is the gigantic, distant cousin of a modern-day chicken!

What prehistoric birds reveal

The chicken is the most common avian dinosaur today. Birds have spread across all continents as successfully as their dinosaur ancestors. More than 10,000 species are currently recognised worldwide. By studying some ancient birds, we can trace similarities to the fearsome dinosaurs we've already seen.

Huge 'terror birds' alive just after the K–T extinction were 2.5 metres tall and presided over the food chain. Out at sea, measuring six metres from wingtip to wingtip, prehistoric pelagornithids were similarly huge and probably had the widest wingspan of any bird that ever lived.

'Turn the page to discover what today's birds have inherited from the dinosaurs!'

DINOSAURS TODAY

Did birds inherit feathers from dinosaurs?

Birds' feathers are an adaptation that first evolved a long time ago, on their dinosaur ancestors! Some early dinosaurs had small quills or 'proto-feathers', perhaps for displaying to attract mates. Some dinosaurs, such as *Haplocheirus*, evolved with branching feathers as well, possibly for keeping warm. *Archaeopteryx*'s feathers may have given it 'lift' to help it glide. Early downy feathers were simple threads, but later feathers were more complex, as species began to flap their wings and started to fly!

ARCHAEOPTERYX
Feathered, Jurassic 'bird-like' dinosaur

FOR FLYING: FLIGHT FEATHER

FOR DISPLAY: PROTO-FEATHER

FOR WARMTH: DOWNY FEATHER

HAPLOCHEIRUS
Feathered, Jurassic dinosaur

Why do dinosaurs and birds have hollow bones?

Like all theropods, *Haplocheirus* and *Archaeopteryx* had hollow bones. This shows dinosaurs had air sacs in their bodies, like birds today, which helped drive air through the lungs and provided extra oxygen for energy. Hollow bones are also much lighter, and like feathers, they may have helped 'in-between' bird-like dinosaurs such as *Archaeopteryx* to glide. Without this inheritance from the dinosaurs, birds would not be able to fly.

DINOSAURS TODAY

CROW
Most intelligent avian dinosaur today

Where might we spot dinosaurs today?

Many dinosaurs were warm-blooded, just like birds. Some ran on two legs like ostriches or had long pointed skulls like crows. Many had beaks that helped them feed. Some dinosaurs had feathered wings that enabled them to fly. In their hips, some dinosaurs had a Y-shaped 'wishbone', a feature only found in birds today. For reasons like these, palaeontologists continue to class birds as dinosaurs, meaning there might be a dinosaur outside your window right now!

OSTRICH
Largest avian dinosaur today

Oviraptorid • Ostrich • Chicken
DINOSAUR EGGS

Do dinosaurs and birds care for their eggs?

From *Pisanosaurus* to *Ankylosaurus*, every dinosaur laid hard-shelled eggs, with oviraptorids laying the largest eggs of all. All birds today lay eggs as well, whether small like a chicken's, or huge like an ostrich's. Most birds build nests to care for their eggs. Some dinosaurs also built bowl-like nests and covered their eggs with twigs or leaves, while others buried them. Certain birds gather in colonies to look after their young, just as some dinosaurs are known to have done.

AGENT EAGLE'S DINOSAUR BRAIN-TEASERS

'We've made it back to the library! In case the club needs to test your knowledge, here are some brain-teasers to sort the average dinosaur dabbler from the expert. Check your answers with HQ - www.eagleexplorer.club.'

THE DATE CONUNDRUM
Unfold the timeline and put the dinosaurs in the correct order, start with the oldest, followed by the most recent.

A. CAUDIPTERYX   **B.** CHICKEN   **C.** PROCERATOSAURUS   **D.** ALVAREZSAURUS

THE NAME GAME
Use the timeline and the clues below to guess the dinosaurs' names.

A. A mythical fiery creature is the inspiration behind this dinosaur's name.

B. This tall dinosaur shares a strong connection with an Ancient Greek god.

C. This dinosaur takes its name from a famous dinosaur hunter.

THE BIG QUIZ

Read my report carefully to discover the answers.

1. **DINOSAUR IDENTIFICATION**
   What makes the leg bones of a dinosaur different from those of other reptiles?

   a) Dinosaur hip bones were twisted like a corkscrew
   b) Dinosaur legs splayed out to the sides
   c) Dinosaur legs always pointed straight down

2. **DINOSAUR LIVES**
   What did Triassic dinosaurs typically eat?

   a) They ate rocks and sand
   b) They ate meat
   c) They ate termites

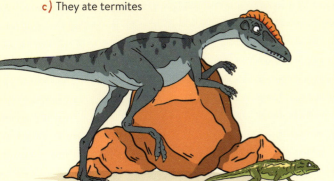

3. **DINOSAUR SURVIVAL**
   How big were the largest dinosaur eggs?

   a) Up to 30 centimetres in diameter
   b) Up to 5 centimetres in diameter
   c) Up to 5 metres in diameter

4. **DINOSAUR DIVERSITY**
   Spinosaurus was probably the largest land predator ever. What was its main source of food?

   a) It ate other *Spinosaurus*
   b) It sunbathed and got its energy from the sun
   c) It caught fish to eat

5. **DINOSAUR EXTINCTION**
   Which of these events do scientists think may have caused the K–T extinction?

   a) A giant meteorite blasting into the Earth from Outer Space
   b) Huge mammals eating the dinosaurs' favourite food
   c) Violent hurricanes

6. **DINOSAUR EXCAVATION**
   What name was given to Othniel Marsh and Edward Drinker Cope's rivalry?

   a) The Fossil Fight
   b) The Bone Wars
   c) The Skeleton Showdown

7. **DINOSAURS TODAY**
   Palaeontologists consider today's birds to be a type of dinosaur. Which of these statements is *false*?

   a) Today's birds have feathers, just like some dinosaurs
   b) Today's birds are warm-blooded, just like some dinosaurs
   c) Today's birds have teeth, just like some dinosaurs

CLUB NOTICES

SPECIAL AGENTS WANTED!!

For reasons we cannot reveal, the Eagle-Eyed Explorer Club is recruiting new agents.

Not everyone will be up to the challenge, but to test if you are really eagle-eyed, crack the code below.

MISSION INSTRUCTIONS

1. Agent Eagle has encrypted a number code into seven red stamps in his journal.
2. Make a note of each stamp's shape and the number it contains.
3. Visit HQ's online portal: www.eagleexplorer.club.
4. Enter the correct numbers into the matching online shapes to break the code.

IF YOU SUCCEED, HQ WILL DO THE REST.

CALLING ALL AGENTS

CLUB RULES

1 Follow your beak! Natural curiosity often leads to the best adventures.

2 Ask questions! As every Explorer knows, there is always more to find out.

3 Don't forget! The real world is far more interesting than anything you can make up.

AQUILA NON CAPIT MUSCAS
THE EAGLE DOES NOT CATCH FLIES

AGENT RENDEZVOUS

Curious to know more about our Explorer missions?

Catch Agent Eagle before he starts his next mission – meet up in person at schools, festivals or workshops.

Contact: **HQ@EAGLEEXPLORER.CLUB**
Codeword: '**EVENT**'

MISSION 01 — DINOSAURS!
MISSION 02 — BUGS!
MISSION 03 — PLANTS!
MISSION 04 — MAMMALS!
EXPLORER MISSIONS

Written by Nicholas Forshaw, Patrick Skipworth and Christopher Lloyd. Illustrated by Andy Forshaw. Designed by Andy Forshaw and Assunção Sampayo. Published by What on Earth Publishing Ltd, The Black Barn, Wickhurst Farm, Leigh, Tonbridge, Kent TN11 8PS, United Kingdom, in association with the Natural History Museum, London. Printed in China by Waiman.

First published in Great Britain in 2017 by What on Earth Publishing. Copyright © 2017. All rights reserved. No part of this publication may be reproduced or transmitted in any form or by any means, electronic or mechanical, including photocopy, recording, or any information storage or retrieval system, without permission in writing from the publishers. Requests for permission to make copies of any part of this work should be directed to info@whatonearthbooks.com.

978-0-9932847-7-9

whatonearthbooks.com